SAVING SADIE

A Border Collie's Journey

Yvette Broussall

Balboa Press books may be ordered through booksellers or by contacting:

Balboa Press
A Division of Hay House
1663 Liberty Drive
Bloomington, IN 47403
www.balboapress.com
1 (877) 407-4847

ISBN: 978-1-5043-4649-8 (sc)
ISBN: 978-1-5043-4650-4 (e)

Print information available on the last page.

Balboa Press rev. date: 01/14/2016

BALBOA.
PRESS
A DIVISION OF HAY HOUSE

I dedicate this book to Sadie, my Soulmate Border Collie who gave me love unconditionally and never left my side. Sadie was so special to me and I will never forget her. I think of her daily. Until we meet again, please wait for me Sadie. I also want to thank Sadie for being such a wonderful Border Collie that inspired me to get more! I currently have Dorsey, Fancy and Scout from Adventure Kennels in Hayden Idaho owned by Sandy Reeves. Sandy helps train with obedience, agility and trick classes.

Acknowledgements:

I want to thank many people who helped Sadie over the years. A big thank you to Cassandra Holmes for posting Sadie on the internet with a beautiful picture of Sadie and letting people know Sadie needed a home and quick! I also want to thank Cassandra for the back and forth emails and the brief talk over the phone about Sadie too.

I also want to thank Pam Sourelis for the animal communication with Sadie and the Reiki healing that she gave her.

I want to thank Marie Cecile for the beautiful artwork of Sadie's soul portrait and the words that Sadie wanted to convey to me.

A special thank you to Shirley Scott, who has given me many sessions of animal communication to help Sadie through the years.

A big thank you to Jill Culver for the lovely painting of Sadie and what she was told by Sadie to convey to me.

Introduction:

I have had many animals in my life, early on and now. All are special but sometimes, you meet one that goes beyond your expectations and steals your heart and soul. Some animals are in your life for different reasons that we don't always understand. While I love all the animals I have had in my life, Sadie is the first one that I had privately cremated. Alaska, was a very large female Samoyed that was rescued and I adopted from a Samoyed rescue in 2000. In 2009, Alaska wanted to be buried at home, and home was in Spring Creek Nevada. Alaska made her wishes known to me via an animal communication session with Val Heart. I did as Alaska requested.

For most of my animals, I chose not keep the remains because either I did not have the money at the time to have a private cremation or I did not feel I could keep all the ashes. I would indeed have many urns if I had. Animals are very important to me and maybe that is why I have had so many of them around me and prefer them to most people. Sadie was so very special to me that I wanted to have her ashes kept in a special urn with her picture on it.

Chapter one Finding Sadie on the internet

On May 15th 2008, I was looking on the internet for dogs and cats in my area. Most people just "look" when they are either really looking for some particular animal or just browsing to pass time. Now, I did not need another animal in the house, as I already had two Samoyeds, Cleatus and Alaska both rescues, Heidi, our over- sized German Shepherd and two Maine Coon cats, Lonny and Jamie. I was just browsing on the internet that day and saw a listing titled Death Row!! and a picture of a happy and a little portly Border Collie with a sweet smile on her face. Her face was black mostly and she had mostly a white body with black ticking on her fur. No name, just Death Row!! She was listed with Monster Rescue in Battle Mountain Nevada about 80.15 miles from Spring Creek one way! So it would be 160.3 miles round trip to get her. I was curious and captivated by her smile and why she was in the shelter. She looked like a happy girl despite her circumstances. It was love at first sight when I saw Sadie! I just wanted to give this special girl a home for her final years of life. Sadie was with me for 6 years. I never asked anything from her. She had no job to do. She was the perfect dog.

Sadie as pictured on internet with Monster Rescue as "Death Row!!" used by permission Cassandra Holmes

The ad listed by Monster Rescue said: This very sweet girl was picked up as a stray and is waiting for someone to take her home from the pound in Battle Mountain. She is very calm and very eager to please! This sweet girl appears to have an injured right eye but appeared to be an old eye injury. The ad also said to please help her find her way home!! If you are interested in adopting this girl, we will pull her from the shelter, have her altered, and vaccinated. Her adoption fee would be $125 unless she was already altered.

I decided to contact Monster Rescue to find out more about "Death Row!!" Here are my original emails:

--- On **Thu, 5/15/08, Yvette Broussal** wrote:

From: Yvette Broussal < >
Subject: Death Row Border Collie
To: xxxxxx@yahoo.com
Date: Thursday, May 15, 2008, 3:34 PM

Wanted to find out more about the Border Collie with the injured eye. Is she good with other dogs and cats? Has she been looked at by a Dr. to see if the eye can be saved? I live in Spring Creek and have 3 dogs. My number is 775-xxx-xxxx.

Where is she located to go visit her?

Thank you for any info.

Yvette Broussal

Here is the response email:

To: Yvette Broussal

Hello Yvette,

I doubt she has had her eye looked at. She is in the local shelter as of now, but is in need of a home. If you have an interest in her, I will take her to get her eye looked at included in the adoption. It isn't life threatening, nor does it look like her eye is any danger of being lost. It has a weird haze as though it maybe an older injury. She has been wonderful with the other dogs at the shelter. Very easy going and lovely girl. Please let me know if you have any further interest.

Thank you
Cassandra

At this point after speaking with Cassandra by phone and getting the number to the shelter, I called the shelter to inquire about this sweet girl. Cassandra did not know at this point I called the shelter and talked to the Animal Officer about "Death Row!!"and would coming the next day to see her. I told the Animal Control officer not to put her to sleep until I had a chance to see her the next day. It was too late in the day to get to Battle Mountain before the shelter closed the day I called. I was the prospective adopter in the following email as Cassandra was unaware I had just spoke with the Animal Control officer at the shelter.

---On Thu, 5/15/08, Yvette Broussal wrote:

From Yvette Broussal
Subject: Death Row Border Collie
To: xxxxxx@yahoo.com
Date: Thursday, May 15, 2008, 7:25 PM

Hi Cassandra,
I emailed my husband about the dog but I have not heard from him today. He works in Idaho at the Sunshine Mine and might be underground today.   Let me see what he thinks about it first. Do you

know if she is good with cats? My dogs have the basement down stairs to themselves and have a large fenced enclosure. My cats are indoor only and stay upstairs and do get along with my dogs. I just did not know if this collie likes to chase cats or is fine with them. I have a really good veterinarian in Spring Creek too. I will let you know more about the possibility of adopting her today. Thanks for the info.

Yvette

To: Yvette Broussal

Hi,

I spoke with animal control and they said she did not mind the two cats that live out there. They do have a prospective adopter. Please keep in touch.

Thanks

Cassandra

From: Yvette Broussal
Subject: Re: Death Row Border Collie
To: xxxxxx@yahoo.com
Date: Thursday, May 15, 2008, 11:06 PM

Hi Cassandra,

I just called the shelter and they said that she does not try to run off or chase cats that they know of. I told them I would come down on Friday to see her. She sounds like a sweet girl! My husband does not mind so... I will let you know.

Thank you for helping all the animals!

Yvette

Chapter Two : Trip to Battle Mountain Nevada to meet Sadie

I was excited that I was to meet with Sadie today. I was unsure of what to expect and did not want to get my hopes up if she did not like me or want to go with me and what about cats??? I left my house in Spring Creek around 9 AM which would get me into Battle Mountain sometime after 10 AM when the shelter opened. The drive was long but I have traveled it many times. I had a map to the shelter since I was not familiar with Battle Mountain as I usually just drive straight through. I have never been at this shelter before.

Upon arriving to Battle Mountain, I found the cross streets and traveled along the road that should take me to the shelter. I had problems finding the shelter or the street since it was not labeled well and my paper map was not zoomed in enough to find" the" street. I just kept travelling on this road back and forth and could not find road to take. I tried calling the shelter, but no answer. In desperation, I found the Chamber of Commerce Visitors Center across the rail road tracts in the opposite direction I needed to go just to find out where I was missing the turn. Upon entering the building, I asked the lady there sitting at a desk, where is the animal shelter? I need to save this dog, and showed her a picture of "DeathRow!!" She told me I was driving in the right area, but said, "You need to go back and take the road off to the right and look for the water tanks. The shelter is out that way, you can't miss it. "I got back in my car headed back to the main road and found the dirt road off to the right. The sign for the shelter was there, but so faded, it was hard to read. I just wanted to get there before something bad happened.

As I drove up to the gravel parking lot of the shelter, I noticed all the kennels faced all the cars coming in to the parking lot. In the very first kennel, there she was! She was jumping and joyful! I was thinking, does she do this type of behavior every time someone drives up? I did not want to get all the dogs going, so I parked on the back side of the shelter and went in. I was thinking I do not want all the dogs in there getting their hopes up if I go in the kennel, so I asked the Animal Control Officer, could you bring me out this dog? I showed her the picture of who I was interested in. I waited as she brought "Death Row!!" out.

Chapter Three: Meeting Sadie

As I waited in the hallway, I was anxious waiting to meet Sadie, only known as "Death Row!! at this point. The lady brings her out, and she was happy and jumping and not even concerned about the one cat in one of the holding cages. That was a good sign! I was told "Death Row!!" is really "Sadie" and she was not claimed by her owners. Apparently, she had been in there before, and a friend to the people who owned Sadie had told them to go get her one time before. I could not believe anyone would leave a sweet dog like Sadie in there longer than needed! How could someone not be looking for her? Sadie was very friendly and sweet as her picture on the internet clearly shows her personality.

I never had a Border Collie before and was concerned since I did not want one who chased cats or wanted to eat them. My fears were unfounded. As I filled out the paperwork to get her, I learned more about Sadie. I found out she was most likely 10 years old since they did have a January 1998 for her age. I really did not have much to go on. How is she was in the house? Or, what home life did she have in her past? I really did not know if she was a working dog for herding or not. I just was told her family did not come for her and she had been there once before.

As I filled out the paperwork, Sadie was very patient to wait. It only cost $15 to bail her out! I do not know what she was thinking at the time but she seemed happy I was there, a very jubilant ten year old dog Sadie was! I knew if I did not take her, the chances of her getting out were slim. All too many dogs that are older do not even get looked at. It is sad to see so many dogs euthanized because of their age. The Animal Control Officer told me that she gave Sadie one week extra since she was such a good dog and did not want to see her die. I was very glad I had a chance to see her when I did because I don't think she had much time left. If it was not for Monster Rescue to post her picture and me not "looking" on the internet the day before, I don't think Sadie would be around to live to a ripe old age of sweet 16. I was fortunate to have the day off to find her and drive out to see her.

Chapter Four: The Ride Home

As I drove back home to Spring Creek, Sadie wasted no time to snuggle in the car! She was really in my lap and nudging me the whole time and making it a challenge to drive in a straight line! She was so sweet and silly! I called my vet in Spring Creek as I got into Elko to see if I could get her in for an exam. I was able to get Sadie in to see the vet as I drove into Spring Creek.

As I filled out the paper work for the vet, Sadie was still happy and not bothered by being in the clinic. As Dr. Moriaty examined Sadie, she recommended blood work, stool sample and looked at the injured eye. Sadie was healthy and just needed some surgery to repair some of the eye tissue around the injured eye. Her right eye had an old injury and had some vision but some tissue around the eye was torn away. So Sadie incurred a $400 bill just that first day! Surgery was another $300 or so. I wanted to help Sadie so it did not bother me to spend money on her since she did not seem to be well cared for by her former owners. I also bought a new blue collar with turtles on in with a matching leash from the clinic. Sadie also got a new toy by Zanies that was a bungie toy with donut shapes at both ends!

As we left the veterinary clinic, Sadie was back to snuggling in the front seat with me. My husband was still working in Idaho at the Sunshine Mine so he had not met Sadie yet. He would be coming home in a few days to see the new family member. I had a few days alone with her and that was good.

Sadie upon entering the house, was greeted by my cats, Jamie and Lonny both Maine Coons. Lonny went right up to Sadie and nudged and head butted her! Sadie did nothing! It was almost like she knew that she had a home and needed to just "be". Perhaps she knew that if she did not get along she would end up in the shelter again. I think Sadie was a very easy going dog and was just happy to be in a place with someone who wanted her and loved her. I think she liked and craved the attention I was giving her! I did introduce her to my other dogs, Cleatus, Alaska, and Heidi who stayed down stairs and had direct access to an enclosed yard. Sadie was friendly and did not cause any upset. Cleatus was too interested in her so I did not want the new family member to be pestered all night while I slept. I decided to let Sadie sleep upstairs with me in bed, when I turned in for the night. We even watched the Dog Whisperer on Animal Planet! Sadie was hogging the couch! What a sweet little snuggler she was! She was a velcro dog but I did not care. Before going to bed, I emailed Cassandra about adopting Sadie. I sent some pictures to her of Sadie too.

From: Yvette Broussal
Subject: Re: Death Row Border Collie
To: xxxxxx@yahoo.com
Date: Friday, May 16, 2008, 9:50 PM

Hi Cassandra,

Well I had to get her! She is so sweet! I got her to my vet as I got into town. Got blood work done, pain meds, eye ointment, and wormer. She also got a new collar treats and a new toy! My cat Lonny walked right up to her and nudged her! My other dogs seem OK with her. My male Samoyed is too interested in her! I think everything will be ok. I have taken some pics. She is a real couch snuggler! We are watching the dog whisperer right now. Thank you for putting her on the Monster Rescue link on the internet.

Yvette

Cassandra responded to me with this email:

To: Yvette Broussal

Oh that is soooo wonderful!! Thank you so much for saving her. Please do keep in touch and I will take her off the site!!
I love the pics!!!
Cassandra

As I turned in for the night, Sadie joined me on the bed. Sadie wasted no time to snuggle me all night! I could not imagine anyone not wanting this sweet Border Collie! She is better company than my husband! Sweet Girl Sadie, snuggle master! She also earned the title "love weasel"!
Here are some pictures I sent Cassandra

Photo of Sadie downstairs on the futon. Photo by Yvette Broussall

Sadie upstairs. Photo by Yvette Broussall

Sadie with toy downstairs. Photo by Yvette Broussall

Sadie with Bandana on. Photo by Yvette Broussall

Chapter Five: A few Days Alone with Sadie

After adopting Sadie we had time to spend together. She never left my side but when she did, she came back as soon as possible. I loved her company! She was good when I took her out. She stayed with me on the property and did not need to be leashed outside while I fed the horses. I would leash her if we took a walk off the property. Sadie did not appear to have a strong herding drive, but it could have been due to being older or just did not care to herd. I did not have a need for a herding dog. I just wanted to save Sadie and give her a home for the remainder of her life on this earth. I wanted her to feel loved and cared for and she was.

Sadie just hung out with me all day upstairs and then I would take her down stairs so she could take a potty break. When I was working on the computer, Sadie was at my side. The computer was down stairs in a room that we chose to be an office. Sadie would go and take her break on her own when she needed to. Sadie was and still is the best dog I ever had adopted. She never caused a problem with the cats or other dogs and was a perfect house guest. I even brought her over to my parent's house in Spring Creek and she was perfect there too even with my parent's two pugs, Jack and Jake. Sadie snuggled with me every night in bed. I waited until my husband got home to finally meet Sadie. I did not want the "snugglefest" to end between Sadie and me.

Chapter Six: My first day of leaving Sadie home by herself

I had to get ready for work on Sunday and my husband was on his way home to stay for a week. I had to leave Sadie home down stairs in an area that we portioned off when we had Heidi as a puppy. I put pee pee pads out for Sadie and knew she might make a mess but I did not want to leave her unattended with the other dogs while I was gone. She was just too new to the household to leave unattended. Sadie did not cause any problems but I did not want Heidi who was 130 pounds to hurt her or Alaska who weighed in at 70 pounds. Alaska was an alpha female and I was not sure if she would attack Sadie either. Cleatus was good for the most part but could be nasty. It was better to be safe than sorry. Sadie would be safe as I left for the mine that day.

Later in the day, my husband called me as I was driving in from the Elko parking lot where I get the bus to and from the mine. I asked how Sadie was doing and found out she got out of her area and was with the other dogs as my husband drove up to the house. I could not figure out how she got out of her area until I saw what she did. Sadie jumped onto the sink area which is a bit high I would think for a 10 year old dog and came down on a small metal table on the other side of the enclosure inside the house! I checked her for any injuries and there was none. She was happily running around with the other dogs. Sadie was very sneaky!

My husband liked Sadie but she would not listen to him. She really liked me so if I asked her to do something she would do it for me and ignore him. I guess she really bonded to me in the first two days I had her to myself.

I tended to go to bed early since I got up early around 3 AM to go to work. Sadie and I turned in early to go to bed and were sleeping and were pretty content. We were both snuggled on the bed. Later, and I heard my husband walking down the hallway to the bedroom and Sadie ran off the bed and charged him! She was growling and showing teeth to him since she did not know him that well yet. I liked the way she at least felt protective towards me, but my husband did not like it. I did tell him if it was a stranger in the house, at least Sadie would try to do something. My husband did not like having Sadie on the bed between us when he went to bed, but I just wanted her to feel loved and comforted while I held her. She stayed on the bed that night and many more to come.

Chapter Seven: Sadie-The Enforcer

After having Sadie in my life for a very short time, she learned the rules of the house. At least as far as what cats were allowed to do or not to do. My cats were always getting into my kitchen cabinets and I did not like having to re-clean pots and pans when they would get into the cabinet. Jamie was the worst offender. Her registered name was "Jamie Jump Up". Jamie was always in the lower cabinets and jumping on the counters. Sadie noticed I was always getting the cats out of the cabinets. Sadie would nudge Jamie or Lonny if they got close to the cabinet or was trying to get in the cabinet. Sadie earned the name "The Enforcer" by her actions. She was always gentle with the cats and never bit them. She just used gentle nudges to remind them not to get in the cabinets or jump on the counters. I really appreciated her help!

I wish Sadie could have helped me in another way. Lonny would steal my dish towels I had draped over the oven handle. He usually took the towel and put it somewhere in the house. I would find them behind the door in rooms or even more dreaded place- the litter box! I wish Sadie could have helped me but many times Lonny would do this while I was at work and he was upstairs. Sadie was down stairs while I was at work because we had a dog door down stairs. I am sure Sadie would have stopped the dish towels from being put into the litter box had she been upstairs during the day.

Chapter Eight: Life with Sadie

Having Sadie in my life has been a love and a joy especially our life in Nevada. Life in Nevada involved my husband and I to work in the local mines in 2008. We both had jobs that had a work schedule of 4 days on, three days off. This allowed for nice hikes in the Lamoille Canyon which had many different hiking trails depending on how long you wanted to hike. I would take my favorite little girl, Sadie on hikes to Lamoille Canyon even if it was a short 2 mile hike just to see the canyon and the U shaped valleys. This was an alpine setting and very beautiful to see. Sadie was good on the leash and she never caused any problems when meeting other dogs. I wish I would have taken more photos of Sadie in the canyon. She seemed to enjoy herself among the beautiful flowers and trees. We would also take shorts trips to other areas in Nevada like Jarbidge. Sadie was happy just to be with me in the house while I cleaned or was doing work on the computer. She was a very nudgy girl and was always reminding me that she was there! She went by many names besides Sadie. Sweet Girl, Soulmate, Girly Whirly, and Sadie Lady were other names I would call her.

Sadie followed me around the house non-stop just to be with me. The only times she was not with me was when I was at work or Hugh took her on bunny rides. The dogs loved bunny rides which involved them thinking there was a bunny running across the road when there was nothing! When bunnies were present, the dogs would bark and Sadie would bark and look for the bunny while putting her front feet on the dashboard. The injured eye did not stop her from seeing the bunny, real or imagined! The time we lived in Nevada was the best years for Sadie. Sadie was 12 when we moved from Nevada to North Idaho. The move was hard on everyone.

Hike in Lamoille Canyon with Sadie, Cleatus and Heidi. Photo taken by Hugh Smith for me!

Sadie hiking in Jarbidge Nevada 2009. Photo by Yvette Broussall

Chapter Nine: Leaving Nevada

After being unemployed since July 2009, we decided to move back to Coeur D Alene Idaho in Late July 2010 to work at the Sunshine Mine. This was a difficult move since we had a tractor, a horse trailer, 2 small trucks, my diesel truck and two horses to move, plus all our belongings not to mention four cats and four dogs. The animals got moved first and we had to stay at my mother in laws house since we did not have a place to have as our own. The move with the dogs and horses took a toll on me since we drove through Montana and I could not drive anymore. I was sick and could not drive the horses anymore and we laid up in Alberton rest stop. We waited for Hugh's mother to meet up with us so Hugh could drive the truck with the horses and Hugh's mother could drive the other truck with the dogs and cats back to her place in Idaho about 70 miles from Coeur D' Alene.

I was not looking forward to staying in my Mother in laws house since I had been in her house before and I knew it would be as bad as it was before. The home was never cleaned and it had soiled carpets from previous animals in the home. I made it for 6 months and wanted to find another place until we could buy for our own. The dogs were ok and the cats stayed down stairs in an empty bedroom. Poor Lexi was attacked by Annie the German Shepard dog that was adopted by Hugh's mother, and I wanted to find another place to stay to avoid more attacks. I felt we deserved a clean place to stay without her dog Annie attacking our dogs and her older border collie Pal. There were just too many dogs in that household.

It took a while to be able to get a loan so we could get our own place. Leaving Nevada brought so much hardship it was hardly worth the move for a job that lasted 3 years and 2 months. The animals had the hardest time. We finally were able to get a rental in Careywood to stay for six months. The dogs had a place they had fenced in and shelter. The dogs did not like it there and Sadie got out one day and we do not know how long she was out. When we arrived back before 5 PM one night she was out walking around. We fixed up the fencing and all was fine for a while. Sadie escaped again and was walking around with blood on her. She tore open her hip area by trying to get out again. We took her to the emergency clinic in Post Falls to get her sutured up. We did not know why Sadie was the only one getting out. Of course Cleatus would be in great danger of getting out at this time since he had no eyes due to Glaucoma. One eye was removed while in Nevada, the other removed while we were living in Careywood. Sadie did come to work with me at the mine and stayed in my office while she healed. She had many people who liked her and visited her often. Danny Groves who was the head Safety Manager would take Sadie for a potty break if I was out doing something or went underground for a bit.

Chapter Ten: Sadie went missing

Sadie escaped one more time and that day was 4/4/2011, I will never forget it. It was around 5 PM getting back from work and she was just missing! We were frantic as we could not find her. It was dark to make it more difficult to find her and we did not know how long she was out for. In desperation, we used our dowsing rods after calling her name failed to bring her back. We did find the direction she went and also found some of her tracks thanks to the dowsing rods. Hugh drove around the area trying to find Sadie and also gave out his business cards in case someone found her.

Needless to say, we did not sleep that night, and the last thing I said was "Sadie, I hope you are with some nice lady to stay with tonight" as I cried for her. The next day at work, I could not concentrate and paid for an urgent ad made by www.ILostMyDoggie.com. I had a photo of Sadie to email them and they make a flyer that you can post in your area and they also call the people living in the area about your lost dog. I had to try something to get her back. I had a reward for Sadie's safe return in the ad too.

One day went by and no Sadie, but we had put flyers up in the area and went to homes to give out the flyer. Some people said they did see her earlier in the day but we did not find her that day. We asked one man outside his home if he had seen Sadie. He had not seen her but would call if he did see her and gave him a flyer.

While working at the mine the next day, a man called the number on Hugh's card or perhaps even the flyer posted the day before, saying that a friend of his may have our dog Sadie. I got the information from him and he told me the lady's name and where her house was at. It was a quite a ways over from where we stayed in Careywood and Sadie did travel far.

After work, we found the dirt road which was before our turn off road and the house, but no one was there. She had a metal sign with Arabian Horses on it and I figured at least she likes high headed horses like me! I had two American Saddlebreds and later I found out that this lady had one Saddlebred as well.

I did not even hear Sadie there. Sadie was in the garage but I did not know it. We left the flyer and a note to call us when the lady got in. A short time later, the lady called and told us to come over and get Sadie. When we arrived Sadie was gone again! The Lady let her out to go potty and Sadie took off to the lady's mother's house across the way. So she called her kids who were over at her mother's house not far from hers and you could see the house from where we were. The lady said she would come with me to get Sadie since we did not know the road to get to the other house. We got to the other house and Sadie was not real concerned to see us! I wanted to spank her but I wanted to kiss and hug her too! We did get her in the car and offered the lady the reward we had posted. She did not want it and I thanked her for keeping Sadie safe while we were searching for her.

Now we had to fix something else up to keep Sadie in. We decided to use a small shed for wood and make a tall gate and board up the one side. She could not dig out since it had concrete flooring. This was not what I wanted for her but she was safe until we finally left the rental as we did not want to get put into a year lease in that horrible place and went back to Hugh's mother's house. We did not want to stay in the rental since I was always having a difficult time breathing there, later found out to have black mold that was undisclosed before we rented. Also we had bats fly in through the fire place chimney and squirrels trying to break in the house. We later found out that the garage/shed had a suicide in the upstairs area which we did not use and that could have been why the dogs did not like it there.

We ended up back in house of my mother in law again only, to stay long enough to get our own place. We were finally able to get a very large home in Rathdrum that was perfect for the dogs. The home had a large attached garage and had a large yard area with grass and a chain linked fence. It had a dog door from the garage to the yard area so the dogs could get out during the day. One bay of the large garage was designated for the dogs with two old sofa's that Hugh's mother was willing the part with. These sofas were old smelly and dirty but perfect for the dogs who could use them. The dogs were at peace now and so was I.

Chapter Eleven: Sadie and her first soul portrait.

I had a soul portrait commissioned by Marie Cecile Gargano which was interesting in that Marie did not know anything about me or where I worked. She actually had my head coming out of the ground surrounded by mountains, a creek, and silver draped over me with many animals that are surrounding me in the portrait. I was working at the Sunshine Mine where big creek goes through the property and has many mountains and trees that surround it. Sadie I would later find out was the Pegasus in my soul portrait.

I had asked Marie if she did animal soul portraits at one of the holistic fairs in Spokane. She said yes. She also said once the animal comes to her in spirit, it is often close to passing away. Well, I wanted a soul portrait of Sadie anyway since Marie does not do them once they pass on, only while they are living. I gave her partial payment to start when Sadie comes to her. Within a week Sadie comes to her! I was hoping it would be later because I was not ready to lose Sadie. On 2/29/2012 she started Sadie's portrait. The number equals to nine which means completion. It was very touching of what Sadie had to say. Here is what Sadie had to say conveyed by Marie.

2/29/2012= 9

Completion
My Beloved mistress, My Beloved Friend,
You truly are my Master for you are the One who has brought me
into being. You and I have traveled far and wide on the river of
Life and we shall continue on doing so even when this body can no
longer house my vibration, for one cannot separate what is
inseparable in the first place and this we are. And when the time
comes for me to discard this shell for good, please know that I shall
always find a way to come back to you and let you know of my

continued love and devotion.

You call me a Soulmate, a good word for I am but an extension of you, created to be of service to no one but you and I am never quite as happy as when I am able to cuddle up to you and bask in the vibration of your love, and the love that I give you is nothing else but a reflection of the Love you hold for me.

As the emerald in my forehead shows, my service is of the Heart, all that you see in me is actually in you, you simply are unaware of it, but I KNOW, I SEE what is hidden deep within your heart and it is my greatest joy to take burdens and sadness off of you. I bring you joy and comfort, and in my paws you find the love that was not given to you as a child and in your lap, I find the very same. Throughout time, I have also been a teacher of unconditional Love to the human part of you and you shall also remember me as a large gray wolf that first came to you in your dreams as a young Indian boy and later on became a trusted companion.

In my true form, I am a Pegasus, and you and I often fly to the stars at night. Sometimes we explore planets and galaxies and sometimes we go to our special place, a beautiful meadow where you rest and reenergize by a stream as I watch over you. As Sadie, I bring balance into your life, I bring peacefulness and calmness when there is restlessness and I help you to escape from the troubles of this earthly life. I bring simplicity to you in the form of Love, when you experience Love, you go into a place of Oneness with all, nothing else matters, problems fade away and life becomes simple.

That is what I am, very simple, I Am.

The butterflies speak of the dance of joy, the joy that fills my heart when I am near you and like the dragonflies, I remind you of the power of Light that is within you.

As you are aware, the time is nearing for me to leave this earth plane, you shall know when it is time and I ask you not to see a death but simply a transformation from one form to another, just like the larvae transforms into the butterfly.

I am the one who inspired you to have this picture done so I could let you know of my love and my gratitude, and you would know me beyond the form you know me under

Look into my eyes, they are a portal for my vibration to come through. Through them, I shall speak to you and you shall feel my never ending love for you. I shall always remain by your side, in one form or another, listen to the whispers of your heart and you shall hear me and feel me though them.

Blessed be my sweetest and beloved friend for all that you have given me and shall give me again

I Am, Sadie

Sadie's portrait is beautiful as you can see. Marie did not know what Sadie looked like or that I called her a Soulmate. I thought it was great that she got the black ticking! I sent a photo of Sadie to Marie after she had done the painting. You can also see the word JOY as someone pointed out to me. Sadie was 14 years old when this was done. She would go another two years before she left this earth.

Joy! Sadie's Soul Portrait Art work was used by permission Marie Cecile.

Sadie's Soul Portrait Art work was used by permission Marie Cecile.

Chapter Twelve: Life from 14 to 16 years of Age

Sadie was an incredible dog but she was a Soulmate to me. As she aged, she would have a hard time walking and just getting around and finally I had to help her get up and down the stairs. I have had many consults with Shirley Scott an animal communicator and medium. We would always check in with Sadie to see how she was doing. Shirley did say that Sadie's heart would go first before she would not eat food anymore. That turned out to really have happened.

While I was looking on Amazon, I came across a book by Jeff Maziarek, called Codi's Journey. It was a very touching book and how Jeff handled the end of life for his beloved Border Collie Codi. I got the book thinking I will only read it after Sadie is gone. Well, that did not happen. I did decide to read the book and it really helped me cope. Jeff inlisted the help of Pam Sourelis, of www.WingedHorseHealing.com. Pam does healings for many animals including dogs, cats and horses. I did have some questions to ask Sadie and so I emailed the questions to Pam to ask Sadie when it was time for her session. I only needed to keep Sadie quiet at the appointed time then Pam would follow up with an email of the session. This is what Sadie had to say during the session:

Hi Yvette.

I had a lovely session with your beautiful girl.

Her energy seemed to be very low. I know you said she is a quiet girl, but she also seemed quite tired.

I explained that you are concerned about her and want to follow her wishes in her final days.

Pam: Yvette said that when she first saw your face, it was love at first sight, and she knew that you belonged to each other.

Sadie: Yes, she is a very special woman.

Pam: How are you feeling?

Sadie: There is a blockage.

I began the Reiki session at that point. My hands were drawn to her belly. I said a prayer for the blockage to pass or to break up or dissolve if possible, but at some point I got the sense that there is some kind of growth in her belly or intestines. It is not a complete blockage, but it is sapping her strength.

She indicated that she does not want any medical intervention.

She also does not want assistance with passing now. But she might want assistance later if she does not pass on her own. She said that you will know. If the pain becomes too great (it is mild now), she would appreciate assistance in passing.

But she would like to spend as much time as possible with you before she leaves.

I asked if she had anything to share with you today.

Sadie: She has a good attitude about life and death. I know she will be sad when I leave--there is a powerful love between us--but I know she will be OK. She will carry our love in her heart.

Pam: She wants to know if you will be coming back.

Sadie: I don't know. But not to her, not now. I will always be with her, but not in that form.

Pam: She has placed an order for a pup next year.

Sadie: Pups are a wonder. If she can also save a poor abandoned soul--like she saved me--that would also be a wonder. It's been a good life. We had a lot of fun together.

Pam: She said that you've always been quiet and calm--unlike most of your breed.

Sadie: Yes? I was just happy to finally be home. There was no reason to jump and shout. I was worn out. But life with her has been a joy. She has been a lot of fun. We have made each other laugh.

I hope that in my last days she will keep her sense of humor. This is my favorite thing about her.

Pam: I will remind her. Peace to you, Sadie.

At this point, I shared my Reiki hands with her for awhile longer before ending the session.

At some point during the session, I got the sense that she might be a bit dehydrated. Does that sound right? You might want to syringe water into her mouth from time to time. Just be careful that it doesn't go down her throat; you don't want her to inhale it.

I could be wrong about her needing this now; she could have been showing me a need that will reveal itself a bit later.

Yvette, I hope these notes are helpful to you and that they bring you peace. Your beloved Sadie loves you dearly. **To say that when she found you she finally came home is about the highest compliment anyone can pay to someone else**.

If you need further assistance, please let me know. I also want to point out my December special to you (below my signature, in pink). Reiki can bring balance, can help to calm the grieving heart.

Be well,

Pam

Pam Sourelis
Reiki - Animal Communication - Neuromuscular Retraining
. . . because healing is possible
WingedHorseHealing.com

Chapter Thirteen: Letting Sadie Go

I finally had to let Sadie go after much thought on January 15th 2014. I took her to Dr. Ridgeway in Post Falls Idaho and she listened to her heart and said, "I don't know how she is staying alive, her heart is beating very uneven and could pass at any time." That's when I remembered what Shirley said about Sadie's heart would go before she stops eating completely. I just looked at Sadie and said "Is it time to go?" She seemed very distant and just wanted to rest. Sadie also would lean to one side and she would also turn in circles at times. She was having more difficulties at this time and I knew it was going to be one of the worst days for me. My beloved friend and companion would have to be at rest until I would meet her again.

We moved Sadie to a massage table to rest and I was with her for a few moments and told her how much I loved her and would miss her. I was crying and was trying to not make her upset by my love for her in a crying form. Dr. Ridgeway finally injected Sadie with the Sodium Barbital and Sadie went to sleep. We put her in a large bag to take her to the place that does cremations onsite not far from the clinic in Post Falls. I did have Sadie's picture on a flash drive to give the man who did the cremations. I picked out an urn with a place for her picture and a short description. It would only take a few days to pick up her ashes. I did buy Sadie roses after this. I would buy one for her and one for me.

I did contact Jill Culver who is a very gifted self-taught artist to do a commissioned soul portrait of Sadie. I gave Jill a down payment of $500 deposit in June of 2014 and just waited until she was ready to do Sadie. I was on a wait list. Jill needed some pictures of Sadie and I sent her a few. Most of the pictures were not high quality for Jill to use but I did find a few more to send her. I told her that Sadie would help her decide which photo to use and I was not worried at all in the choice of picture used or timing of the painting.

It was on November 20th of 2014 Jill contacted me that she was ready to do Sadie and I was just let go of contract job I was doing in Utah. So the timing was interesting. I knew there would be some delays due to the timing of the holidays and figured sometime next year Jill would have the portrait done.

The holidays were not the same without Sadie. I would always give her some table scraps to encourage her to eat more. I would cook special meals for her in her last days since she lost so much weight. She would "hide" under the table to get extras. I loved cooking for her.

I was crying for Sadie during the night on February 17th and listening to the song I would play for her. The song was called "Requited Trust" by Stuart Jones on the Animal Healing CD. It had a piano at the beginning of the song and thru ought the song. Little did I know, Jill would email me about Sadie's portrait the next morning. Sadie's portrait was done on February 18th 2015. Timing was everything. Jill did not know about anything about the song and could not wait for her to send me the painting and do a skype session with her.

The Skype session with Jill was on March 1,st 2015 at 9:30 AM. I received my painting on February 27th and was told not to open it yet. Funny thing since Sadie's soul portrait by Marie was done on February 29th 2012 this one would have been around the same time if this was a leap year being on March 1st for the portrait with Jill. See, timing was perfect. When I opened the painting, I was in awe at the likeness that Jill captured of Sadie. It was almost life sized and I could almost put my hands out and hold Sadie's chin in my hands! I cried because it was so beautiful! Jill even put a dog collar at the bottom of the painting to give it a 3-D look with a heart shaped tag! After talking with Jill, I thanked her for her time and asked if I could use her portrait of Sadie since I was writing a book. Jill said yes and I would include contact information so others could ask for a soul portrait to be commissioned of their special pet.

On March 6th, Jill asked one more thing. She sent me an email about what Sadie said- "Thank you for the Piano." She asked if that made sense to me and I said Yes! I used to play a song for Sadie that had a piano at the beginning of the song. Jill did not know that at all. I converted the song so Jill could hear it on her computer as an mp3. I did not know Sadie understood what a piano was! At least she liked the song too!

Sadie's Soul Portrait by Jill Culver used by permission.

Sadie Christmas 2012 the photo used for the soul portrait. Photo by Yvette Broussall

Sadie picked the last Christmas picture I had of her. I did take pictures of her in December of 2013 but not in front of the Christmas tree. Her health was in decline and we both lost our jobs in October of 2013 so not much of a Christmas for 2013. Sadie had vestibular disease and seizures. This caused her to turn in circles until she stopped and would eventually lie down. It seemed to have started when Sadie escaped while in Careywood and got hurt on her hip area and caused some nerve damage. It was fitting that Sadie helped Jill pick out the photo she wanted me to remember her by.

Chapter Fourteen Animal Communication with Sadie.

Over many years, I used many different people to find answers for my animals that I had concerns with. I used Val Heart for a session with Sadie once. She told me Sadie had me wrapped around her little paw! She also said that Sadie had bitten someone but not to be mean and thought someone might have been trying to tease her or something. She was never nippy with me but I was aware that border collies could be this way. Sadie was a perfect dog in the house and everywhere I took her. I never had issues with her in anyway.

I also used Shirley Scott many times. Her website http://www.shirley-scott.com/ has contact information and rates. She is always helpful and sometimes has helped me on short notice many times. Shirley was very helpful with trying to convey what Sadie needed or what she was going through or felt. She was also the one who said Sadie's heart would go before she would stop eating completely. I would even ask before I got Dorsey my male Border Collie if Sadie would come back to me as one of the puppies from Sandy Reeves, a local Border Collie breeder and trainer in Hayden Idaho. I was told no, she would not be back as a puppy for me at least for a while.

I did have Dorsey in August 2013 before Sadie left this earth in January 2014. He was kept behind a baby gate as a puppy so he would not bother her. She was very fragile with her health declining. I really did not plan having a puppy while she was still living but it worked out that way. I really never knew how long Sadie would be with me day to day. Sadie would have good days and bad days, so she really could have gone on her own at any time. As stated before, Sadie would circle and lean to one side, then finally lay down. She also had seizures and would stumble. It was heartbreaking to watch but then she would settle and be OK for a while.

Chapter Fifteen Sadie Sightings

It was hard for me when I lost Sadie. She was everything to me. Sadie was my soulmate. Sometimes my husband would say he would hear a dog walking on the tile toward the front door of the house and no other dogs were in the house or they were asleep on the sofa basically just Dorsey was the only dog allowed in the house. My husband would also have nudges on his leg when he was putting steaks out and he would be standing by the sink. I was working in Utah at the time so I was not in the house much for 2014. He said he felt a nudge while getting a steak out of the packaging by the sink and looked down and saw nothing. Dorsey was on the sofa sleeping. I asked him what side did he get nudged and he said the right side. That was Sadie's favorite side to nudge me on.

On another occasion, I was home for a short time and I went to hear a talk in Hayden so I was out of the house. I had my husband drop me off and he was in the house alone with Dorsey. When it was time to have him pick me up I called him and he was about to leave the house. He said he had let Dorsey out to go to the bathroom and when he was walking past the stairs in the house he noticed something black and white running downstairs but thought it was the our black and white Maine Coon Darla but he realized that it was not as the cats were all downstairs behind the door in the basement. They could not have gone through the door! It happened so fast but Sadie would run downstairs when she was able to. She was known as the Phantom Pooper! She did not want to wake me up to go outside so she would go downstairs and would pee and poop on the carpet! I really did not mind if she woke me up to go do her business outside.

In 2014, on another occasion, I went in to a business and waited for some work to be done. After talking to the person helping me, we got to talking about dogs and different breeds and the person said "Oh that dog in your car". I said what does the dog look like? The person said "Well, I don't know." I said I did not have a dog in my car that day. I later followed up with Shirley on this and she said Sadie was in the car with me that day. The person just saw the energy not a true dog in the car. Sadie did say she would always find a way to come back to me or let me know of her presence according to Marie.

In another "sighting" during 2014, I was at an event in San Diego California in late November. During this event, participants would get a chance to sit in the "hot seat." The "hot seat" a chair, was placed in the front of the room, right next to another chair for the person leading the event. Each "hot seat" session would give each person a message to help them at soul level. There were six candles in total, lit around the room. Three were on a small table in the front part of the room, off to the right side. The other three candles were placed on the tables shaped like a horseshoe facing the front of the room. There was one lit candle per table, where all 8 of us were seated.

When it was my turn to sit in the "hot seat," the message that was given to me was simple. In short, it was to remember joy and to keep my internal flame lit. While the channeling message was being delivered, I was crying and thinking of Sadie. I wanted her with me. All of the participants were sitting with their eyes closed in a meditative state. At the end of the channeling, ALL the candles were extinguished! Candles went out from time to time during the event but never all at once! Usually one or two candles would go out and be replaced with new candles. Everyone gasped! Not one of the other participants had ALL the candles go out during their "hot seat" session.

The other people also felt that another presence was in the room. One person said she felt a nudge on the right side of her arm! Sadie always nudged me from the right side! I am sure Sadie was with me on the trip. During this trip, Jill Culver emailed me about starting Sadie's Soul portrait as stated earlier in this book. The message of Joy reminded me of the message Marie gave me on the Soul portrait of Sadie on pages 24 and 25.

Photo Gallery

Sadie in the snow in Nevada. Photo by Yvette Broussall

Sadie's picture as posted on internet with Monster
Rescue used by permission Cassandra Holmes

09/12/2011

Sadie groomed in 9/2011. I'm A Pretty Girl! Photo by Yvette Broussall

Sadie with her pink hat on. Photo by Yvette Broussall

Recommended sources for help with pets and other services

Shirley Scott: http://www.shirley-scott.com/ - Clairvoyant, Animal Communicator, and Medium.

Pam Sourelis: http://wingedhorsehealing.com/ Professional Reiki practitioner, Animal Communicator, practitioner of Neuromuscular Retraining, writer, and teacher.

Jill Culver: http://www.jillculver.com/ Soul Portraits for Pets and People

Marie Cecile: http://www.mariececile.com/index.html Soul and DNA Portraits

Recommended Books
Codi's Journey by Jeff Maziarek You can buy this on Amazon.com

Other Recommendations:

Breeder for Border Collies:

Adventure Kennels - Champion AKC Border Collies - Sandy Reeves Owner and Trainer in Hayden, Idaho

Website: www.dogtrainingandbreeding.com   Phone and email contact on website.

Training Books: These are but a few, but I like these books!

Understanding Border Collies, by Barbara Sykes available on Amazon.com

Barbara Sykes' Training Border Collies, by Barbara Sykes available on Amazon.com

Collie Psychology, by Carol Price available on Amazon.com

The Ultimate Border Collie, edited by Alison Hornsby available on Amazon.com

Websites on Border Collies:

https://www.bordercollies.com/   Books and gifts about and for Border Collies and owners

http://thebordercollieshop.com/main.sc   Gifts and products about Border Collies

http://www.bordercollie.org/basics/living.html   Information about Border Collies

A short Poem about Sadie

Love and Joy!

Searching, I found black and white

Black and white was shaped into a dog

Only known by the name of "Death Row"

I had to inquire!

Your smile was captivating and eyes filled with joy!

I needed to find out more, before it was too late

When we met, it was love at first sight!

Your joy filled the building

Your love filled my heart

You needed rescue, I heard your call

Your real name was Sadie

Eager to be loved and cherished

I found you before you perished

A soulmate named Sadie

I will never forget you

I will love you forever

Printed in the United States
By Bookmasters